Usborne STEM

ENGINEERING
Scribble Book

THE INVENTIONS IN THIS BOOK WERE SCRIBBLED BY:

Written by
**EDDIE REYNOLDS
& DARRAN STOBBART**

Illustrated by
PETRA BAAN
Designed by
Emily Barden

Series editor **Rosie Dickins**

Series designer **Zoe Wray**

Additional design by **Holly Lamont**

Expert advice from
PROFESSOR SHANNON CHANCE
from the Centre for Engineering Education
at University College London

CONTENTS

Learn to draw in 3-D.

Program a robot to build cakes.

Design a machine to clean up litter in space.

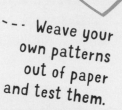

Weave your own patterns out of paper and test them.

Design high-tech clothes to protect hikers in the rainforest.

WHAT IS ENGINEERING?

Engineering means using SCIENCE and TECHNOLOGY to solve problems, often in ways that change the world. Engineering can mean IMPROVING technology that already exists, or INVENTING something completely new.

Engineering is done by ENGINEERS...

MECHANICAL ENGINEERS

Design and build machines, from cars and trains to boilers for heating homes.

CIVIL ENGINEERS

Design and build towns and cities, from bridges to buildings, and roads to railways.

BIOMEDICAL ENGINEERS

Apply engineering ideas to medicine, to create more effective treatments, including designing and building artificial limbs.

AEROSPACE ENGINEERS

Design and build things that fly, including planes and space rockets.

ELECTRICAL ENGINEERS

Design and build systems that allow electricity to be used in everyday life.

COMPUTER ENGINEERS

Design and build computers and their components, and write the software needed for them to run.

Whatever they specialize in, all engineers have to think CREATIVELY.

4

WHAT'S IN THIS BOOK?

Most engineers start out by scribbling ideas and designs on paper. In this book you'll be solving problems in the same way engineers do, with plenty of things to...

DESIGN

BUILD

SOLVE

Imagine

INVENT

TEST

WHAT WILL YOU NEED?

Mostly you will only need this book and a pencil. Occasionally, you might need glue or sticky tape and scissors.

USBORNE QUICKLINKS

To download copies of the templates in this book, and for links to websites with more engineering experiments, go to www.usborne.com/quicklinks and type in the keywords: **scribble engineering**. Please follow the online safety guidelines at the Usborne Quicklinks website.

GOOD IDEA!

Most engineering projects start with a PROBLEM that needs a SOLUTION.

 Ice cream melts too fast

 Bathroom gets flooded

 Muddy dog

Messy car

 Sleeping through alarm

Pick one of THESE probems, OR find your own.

Engineers use a process called **CONCEPTUALIZATION** to help them invent possible solutions.

Try these conceptualization techniques...

WORD CHAINS

Write down the key words that describe your problem, then write down the words that each key word brings to mind. It might spark ideas.

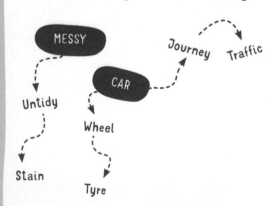

BREAK IT DOWN

Split your problem into SMALLER PARTS. The technical term for this is MORPHOLOGICAL ANALYSIS.

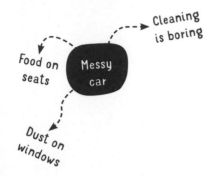

Cleaning is boring

Food on seats

Messy car

Dust on windows

PREVENT THE PROBLEM

Can you think up ways to STOP each part of the problem from happening in the first place?

Pull-out tables to eat on?

Fans that detect dust and blow it away?

DEAL WITH THE RESULTS

If you can't prevent the problem, can you invent ways to DEAL WITH IT once it's happened?

Self-cleaning windows?

Robot that crawls around the car and sprays stain remover?

MAKE AN UPGRADE

Do any solutions ALREADY EXIST? If so, can you think of ways to make them even BETTER?

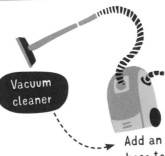

Vacuum cleaner

Add an extra hose to clean twice as fast.

YOUR MASTERPIECE

Combine your ideas to come up with an invention to solve your problem. Scribble it below, and label all the parts with a quick explanation of what each one does.

NAME OF INVENTION: _

INVENTED BY: _

SOLVES THE PROBLEM OF: _

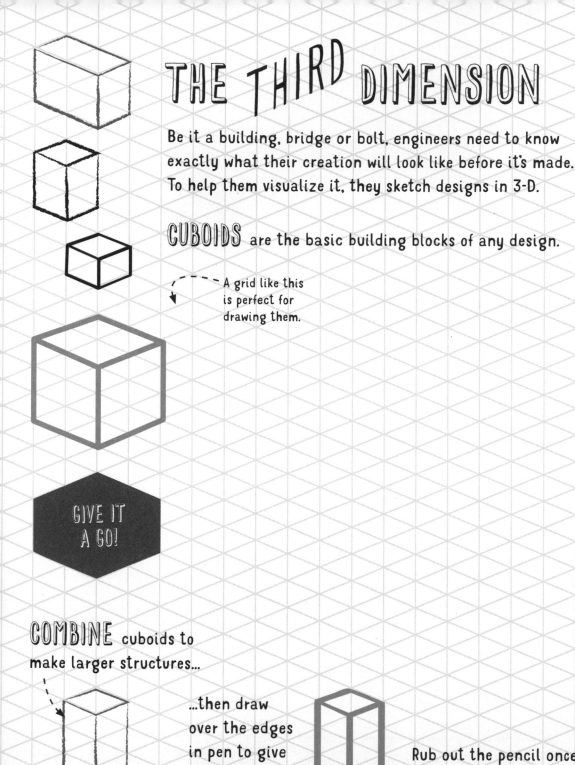

THE THIRD DIMENSION

Be it a building, bridge or bolt, engineers need to know exactly what their creation will look like before it's made. To help them visualize it, they sketch designs in 3-D.

CUBOIDS are the basic building blocks of any design.

A grid like this is perfect for drawing them.

GIVE IT A GO!

COMBINE cuboids to make larger structures...

...then draw over the edges in pen to give the structure DEFINITION.

Rub out the pencil once the ink has dried to make the sketch neater.

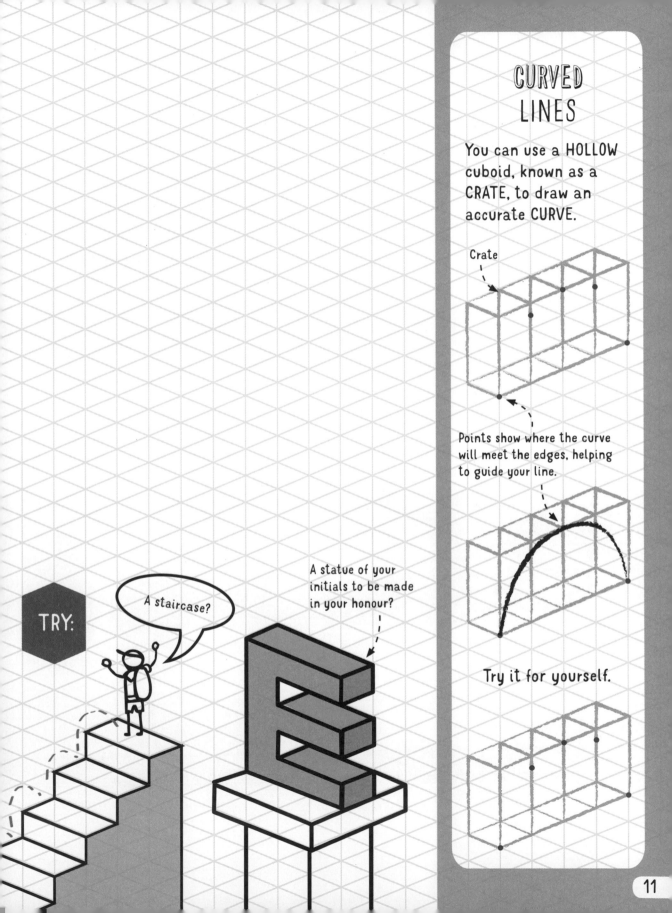

CURVED LINES

You can use a HOLLOW cuboid, known as a CRATE, to draw an accurate CURVE.

Crate

Points show where the curve will meet the edges, helping to guide your line.

Try it for yourself.

TRY:

A staircase?

A statue of your initials to be made in your honour?

11

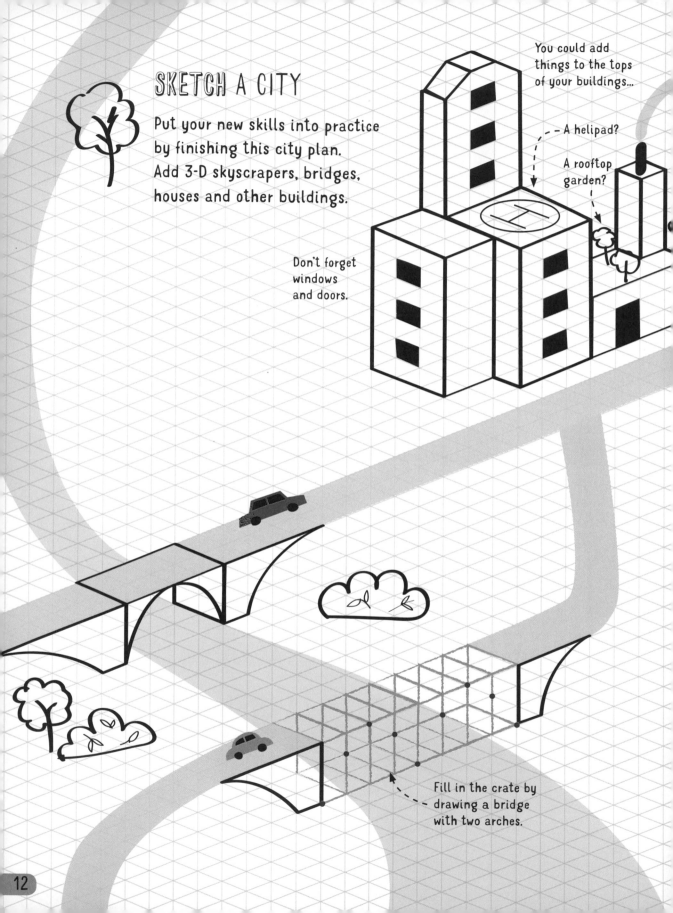

SKETCH A CITY

Put your new skills into practice by finishing this city plan. Add 3-D skyscrapers, bridges, houses and other buildings.

You could add things to the tops of your buildings...

- A helipad?

A rooftop garden?

Don't forget windows and doors.

Fill in the crate by drawing a bridge with two arches.

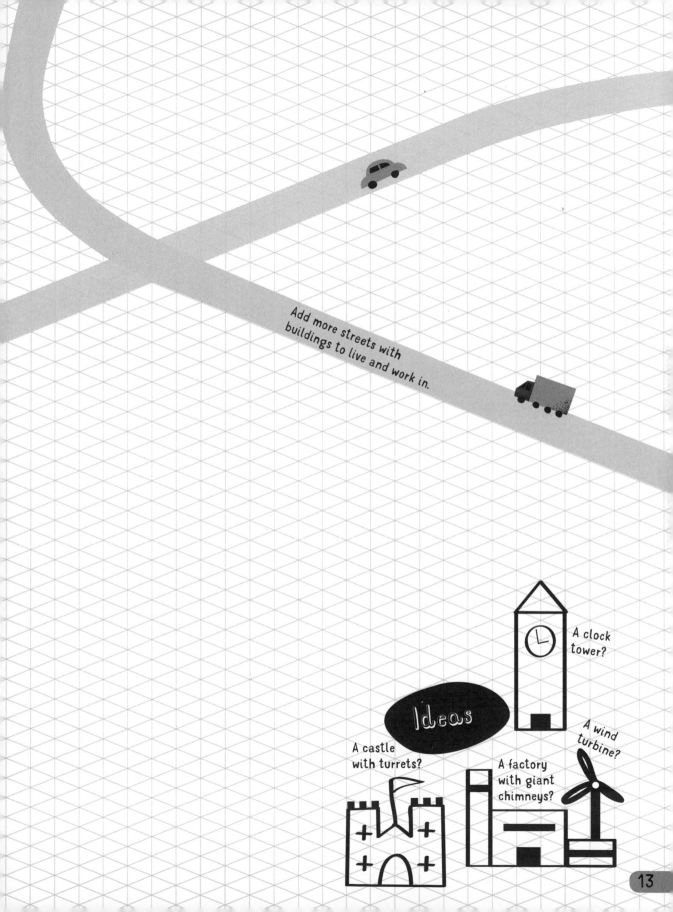

Add more streets with
buildings to live and work in.

Ideas

A clock
tower?

A castle
with turrets?

A wind
turbine?

A factory
with giant
chimneys?

COLLAPSING COLUMNS

The purpose of COLUMNS in a building is to support
the weight above them without BUCKLING.

The weight placed on a column spreads out to its EDGES and CORNERS.
The more EVENLY the weight is spread, the STRONGER the column.

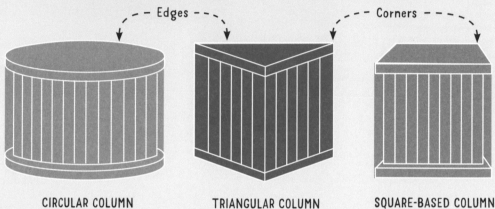

- - Edges - - -   - - - Corners - - - -

CIRCULAR COLUMN   TRIANGULAR COLUMN   SQUARE-BASED COLUMN

Which of the columns above do you predict is the STRONGEST?

BUILD IT: Copy the template on the next page, or print it from the Usborne QUICKLINKS website. Use the strips to make three short columns.

TEST IT: Place this book and then other similar-sized books, one at a time, flat on top of each column, until it collapses. Which column supports the most?

Shape	Number of books
CIRCULAR	_ _ _ _ _ _ _ _ _ _ _
TRIANGULAR	_ _ _ _ _ _ _ _ _ _ _
SQUARE-BASED	_ _ _ _ _ _ _ _ _ _ _

Turn to page 76 for an explanation.

STICK HERE

STICK HERE

STICK HERE

FOLD

FOLD

CIRCULAR COLUMN
(NO FOLDS)

TRIANGULAR COLUMN
(THREE FOLDS)

SQUARE-BASED COLUMN
(FOUR FOLDS)

FOLD

FOLD

FOLD

FOLD

FOLD

CUT

CUT

STICK HERE

STICK HERE

STICK HERE

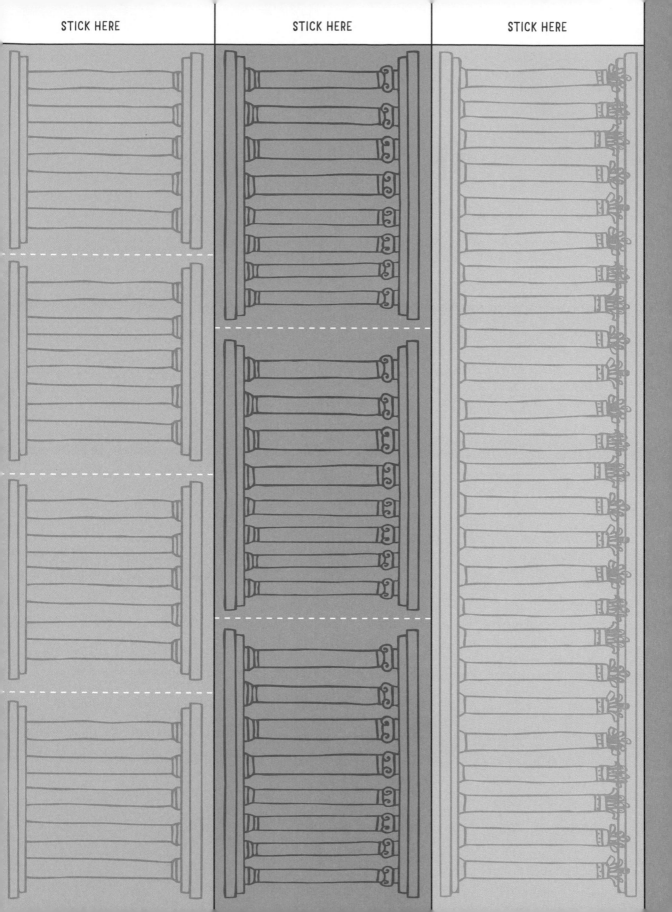

COGS in the machine

Cogs are wheels with TEETH around the edge. When these teeth MESH together, cogs can turn each other. Engineers connect different parts of machines with them.

Tooth

When meshed together, one cog will turn CLOCKWISE and the other ANTICLOCKWISE.

The larger the cog, the more teeth it has and the faster a smaller cog will turn to KEEP UP.

THINK LIKE AN ENGINEER:

Which way does the **FIRST** cog need to turn to lower the cheese?

CLOCKWISE or ANTICLOCKWISE?

Clockwise

Anticlockwise

Mmm, cheese.

TIP: Starting at the bottom, draw arrows on the cogs to show which way they need to turn.

For the answer turn to page 76.

OH, SO SIMPLE

There are six SIMPLE MACHINES that make an engineer's life a lot easier, by reducing the effort it takes to PUSH, PULL and LIFT things.

WHAT IS A MACHINE ANYWAY?
It's a device or tool that performs a physical task.

WHEELS roll, making it easier to move things around.

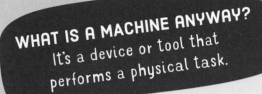

Rod (or axle) connects wheels.

A PULLEY makes it easier to LIFT and LOWER things.

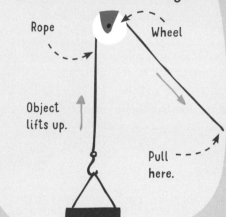

Rope

Wheel

Object lifts up.

Pull here.

LEVERS tilt about a fixed point to help LIFT things.

Push down here.

Object lifts up.

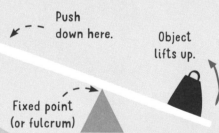

Fixed point (or fulcrum)

An INCLINED PLANE (or ramp) makes it easier to move things up and down.

Pull from above.

Push from below.

WEDGES split things or hold things in place. Axes and doorstops are wedges.

A SCREW can drill through solid materials, and fasten things in position. You twist them in and out of position.

Turn to page 76 to see some possible solutions.

Can you scribble in a simple machine to complete each of the scenes below?

Add a simple machine to help MOVE these bananas UP into the van.

This crane needs to LIFT this ship out of the water.

A simple machine to CUT this watermelon in half?

BEFORE

When the stripy gymnast lands, the other one needs to be LIFTED up.

AFTER

Sketch what will happen after the stripy gymnast lands.

19

EXPLOSIVE ENGINES

First developed in the 19th century, the INTERNAL COMBUSTION ENGINE is a machine that converts fuel into movement.

Inside a car...

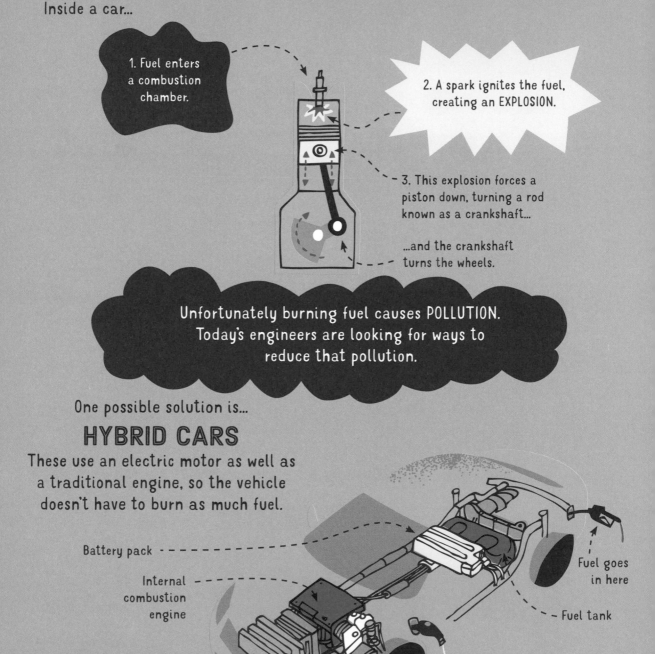

1. Fuel enters a combustion chamber.

2. A spark ignites the fuel, creating an EXPLOSION.

3. This explosion forces a piston down, turning a rod known as a crankshaft...

...and the crankshaft turns the wheels.

Unfortunately burning fuel causes POLLUTION. Today's engineers are looking for ways to reduce that pollution.

One possible solution is...

HYBRID CARS

These use an electric motor as well as a traditional engine, so the vehicle doesn't have to burn as much fuel.

Battery pack

Internal combustion engine

Electric motor

Fuel goes in here

Fuel tank

Battery charger

MAKE IT HYBRID

Can you design a hybrid vehicle here that uses another source of power as well as a traditional engine? Use the suggestions below or come up with your own ideas for new types of power.

Wind turbines...

Pedal power...

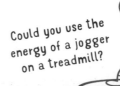

Could you use the energy of a jogger on a treadmill?

BUILDING BRIDGES

Even though you can't see it, a bridge BENDS and SQUEEZES together whenever a vehicle drives over it.

WHAT'S HAPPENING?

WEIGHT
from a vehicle pushes DOWNWARDS, causing COMPRESSION and TENSION.

COMPRESSION
(shown in RED) SQUEEZES the top layer of the bridge inwards.

The weight also spreads to and COMPRESSES the legs.

TENSION
(shown in BLUE) STRETCHES the bottom of the bridge outwards.

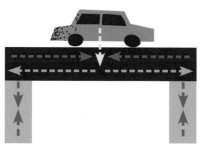

With a bigger weight, the tension and compression get BIGGER too.

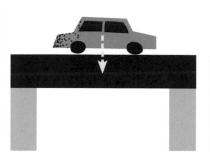

But if the tension and compression become TOO BIG, the bridge will...

COLLAPSE

BUCKLE

SNAP

There's a LIMIT to how much tension and compression each part of a bridge can withstand. This is known as its ELASTIC LIMIT.

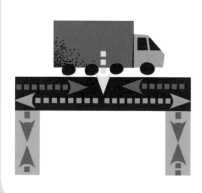

Some bridges have extra supports underneath to SPREAD OUT the impact of the weight.

Suspension bridges have extra supports above.

Adding extra supports helps to avoid reaching the elastic limit for any one part of a bridge.

BUILD YOUR OWN:

Test some different paper bridge designs using the template below. You can copy it, or download it from the Usborne QUICKLINKS website.

Turn the page to record your results.

EXPERIMENT:

1. Place the flat template as shown in the diagram to the right. Load it with small objects of the same size (such as coins or toy bricks) one at a time, until it collapses. How many can it support?

2. Fold up the sides along the WHITE dotted lines and try again. How many of your item can it support now?

3. Fold along the remaining BLACK dotted lines to make a zigzag. How many can it support now?

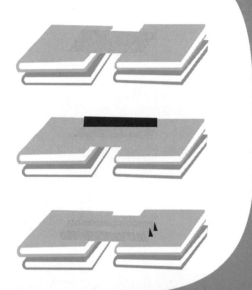

BRIDGE TEMPLATE

How many objects?

BRIDGE 1 _ _ _ _ _ _ _ _ _ _ _ _ _ _ _ _ _

BRIDGE 2 _ _ _ _ _ _ _ _ _ _ _ _ _ _ _ _ _

BRIDGE 3 _ _ _ _ _ _ _ _ _ _ _ _ _ _ _ _ _

Which bridge was strongest?   1 / 2 / 3

Which was weakest?   1 / 2 / 3

Turn to page 77 to see what we found.

One of the strongest paper bridges ever made was built by a student for a school physics project.

It was made out of tape, glue and 90 SHEETS of ordinary paper...

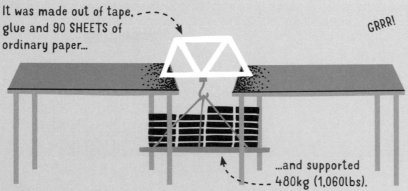

...and supported 480kg (1,060lbs).

GRRR!

That's about the same weight as two adult grizzly bears.

WATER, WATER EVERYWHERE

It's up to engineers to find ways to transport water from natural sources to cities and homes.

How would you get water to the city from the sources below?
Scribble in pipes connecting each one
to the route it needs to take.

HILLY TERRAIN
How would an engineer get the water from this lake to flow over the hills?

UNDERGROUND RIVER
How could you link it to the city?

CANYON
What's the best way to get water across?

POLLUTED WATER
How could you clean it up?

TUNNELS AND PIPES carry water through the ground.

AQUEDUCTS are bridges that carry water across deep ravines.

WATER TREATMENT WORKS have ways to make water safe to drink.

Water naturally flows downwards, but **PUMPS** can reverse the flow.

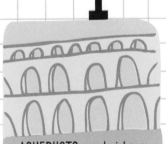

There are answers on page 77.

In some cities, water flushed down the **TOILET** goes to a water treatment works, then back to homes as **DRINKING WATER**.

ON THE MOON

The moon is an ideal place from which to EXPLORE SPACE. However, if people were to build a base there, they would need to overcome a lot of problems first.

DANGERS FROM SPACE

The surface of the moon is at risk from asteroid strikes and deadly radiation.

SOLUTION:

Build UNDERGROUND. The thick rock and dust that make up the moon's surface offer protection.

HOT AND COLD

On the moon, a day lasts around two Earth weeks, followed by a two-week night. There are SWELTERING temperatures during the day, and FREEZING temperatures at night.

SOLUTION:

Solar panels to harvest energy, storing it in batteries to power cooling and heating systems.

IT'S DUSTY

The moon's surface is covered in moon dust which can damage equipment.

SOLUTION:

Moon dust contains a lot of iron, which is attracted to magnets. Magnets could be used to remove the dust from astronauts' spacesuits before the astronauts return to the base.

Design your own underground moon base below. What would it need?

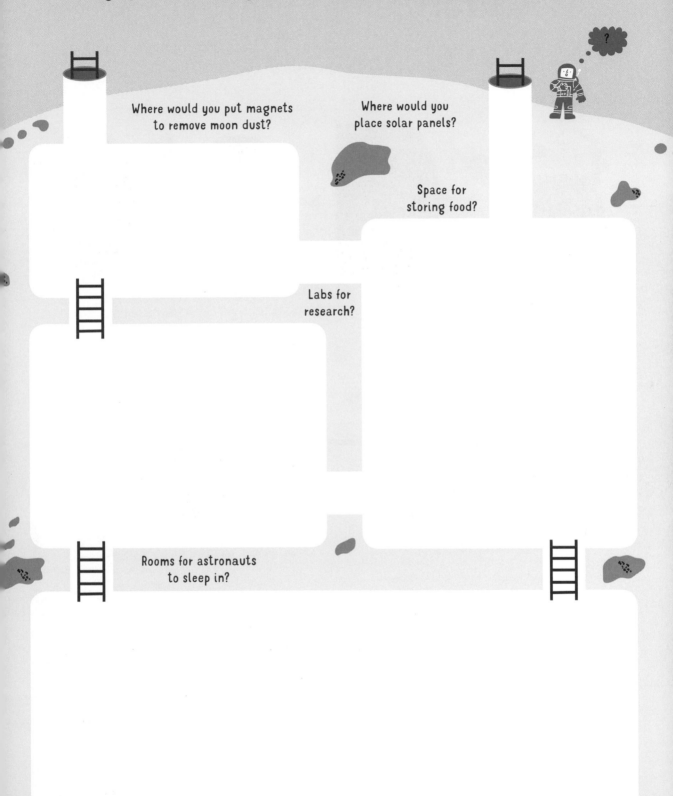

Where would you put magnets to remove moon dust?

Where would you place solar panels?

Space for storing food?

Labs for research?

Rooms for astronauts to sleep in?

INSPIRED BY NATURE

Sometimes, when engineers are trying to find a creative new way to solve a problem, they take inspiration from the world of nature.

NATURE   INVENTION

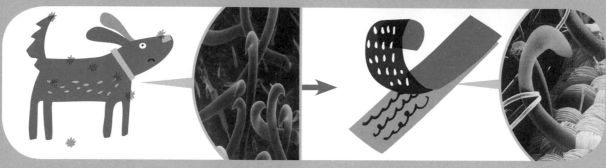

Burdock seeds use tiny hooks to attach to the fur of passing animals.

This was the inspiration for Velcro®, which is used as a fastener all over the world.

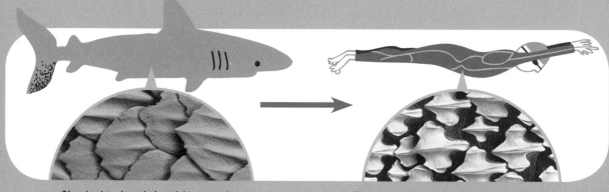

Shark skin has lots of tiny scales which cut through the water.

These scales inspired a scaled swimsuit so good it was banned from the Olympics.

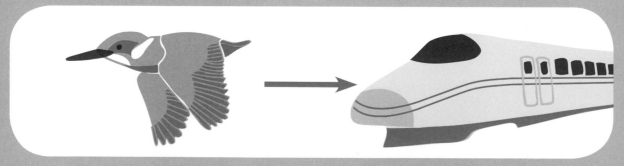

The shape of a kingfisher's beak helps the bird fly more smoothly.

Japanese engineers copied the shape for the front of a high-speed 'bullet' train.

Taking inspiration from the natural world,
can you invent a device to tidy your bedroom?
There are some ideas below to get you started.

Chameleons have long
sticky tongues...

...could you use
something like that
to pick up mess?

Bats make clicking
sounds to help find
things in the dark...

...could you use something
like it to find lost things
under your bed?

Cactuses have
sharp spines...

...could you use
something like them on a
device to collect stray socks?

UNDERSEA EXPLORER

Engineers write programs for robots to explore the ocean depths.

Robots can't do anything without a precise set of INSTRUCTIONS, known as a PROGRAM.

COMMANDS in a program tell a robot to do one thing...

Speed up

Turn left

Pick up object

Using the command symbols given, can you program the robot below to swim to the shells in this sea cave?

COMMANDS

→ Swim one square forward

↻ Make a quarter turn downwards

↺ Make a quarter turn upwards

START

PROGRAM:

The answer is on page 77.

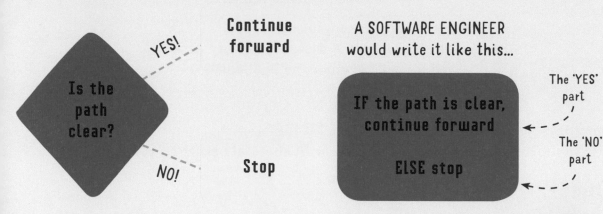

DECISIONS ask a robot a YES/NO question.

Is the
path
clear?

YES! ---- Continue
forward

NO! ---- Stop

A SOFTWARE ENGINEER
would write it like this...

IF the path is clear,
continue forward

ELSE stop

The 'YES'
part

The 'NO'
part

Scribble your own shell, then fill in the DECISIONS
in the yellow boxes below to help the robot identify
and collect it from the cave.

For example...

If the shell
is white,
collect it

Else leave it

This will make the
robot collect only
WHITE shells.

Multicoloured?

Spiral?

Spikey?

Star-shaped?

Patterned?

Smooth?

COLOUR	TEXTURE	SHAPE
If the shell is	If the shell is	If the shell is
- - - - - - - - - - - - -	- - - - - - - - - - - - -	- - - - - - - - - - - - -
collect it	collect it	collect it
Else leave it	Else leave it	Else leave it

ROBO-CHEF

Sometimes software engineers make MISTAKES when writing a program. A mistake is known as a BUG, and fixing it is known as DEBUGGING.

The program below is for a robot in a CAKE FACTORY.
It tells the robot to make a chocolate cake with chocolate stars on top.

PROGRAM:

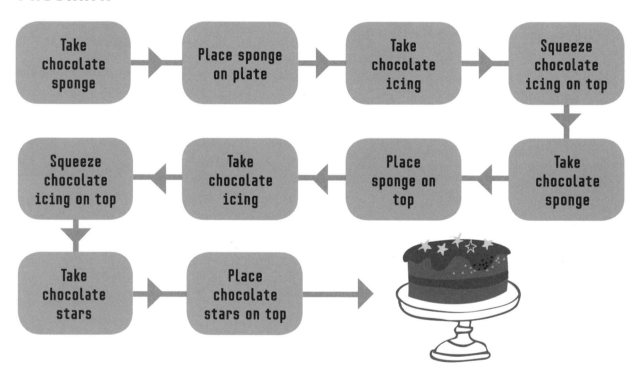

Take chocolate sponge → Place sponge on plate → Take chocolate icing → Squeeze chocolate icing on top

Squeeze chocolate icing on top ← Take chocolate icing ← Place sponge on top ← Take chocolate sponge

Take chocolate stars → Place chocolate stars on top →

Any **BUGS** in the program will make an incorrect cake...

Instructions in the WRONG ORDER

Including the WRONG INGREDIENTS

YUK!

Words typed incorrectly and words the robot doesn't know will make the robot...

STOP!

Here's a new program for a plain sponge cake with jam and cream in the middle, and berries on top.

PROGRAM:

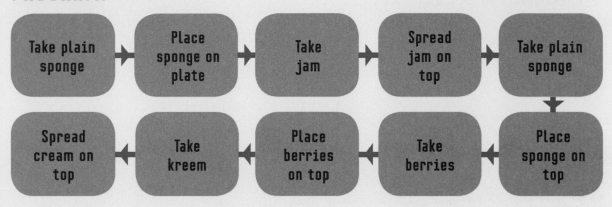

| Take plain sponge | → | Place sponge on plate | → | Take jam | → | Spread jam on top | → | Take plain sponge |

| Spread cream on top | ← | Take kreem | ← | Place berries on top | ← | Take berries | ← | Place sponge on top |

Unfortunately it has some bugs...

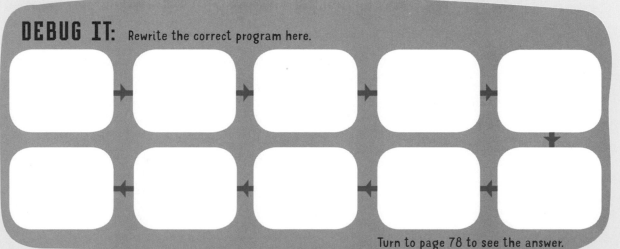

TEST IT: Follow the program, and draw each layer in this box.

Mark the errors as you find them.

DEBUG IT: Rewrite the correct program here.

Turn to page 78 to see the answer.

YOUR TURN

Imagine your OWN cake and draw it.
Then write a program for a robot to build it.

Some engineers program robots to create patterns and words in icing.

CAKE NAME: _

Ingredients

Marshmallow icing?

Rainbow sprinkles?

Edible glitter?

Mini meringues?

PROGRAM:

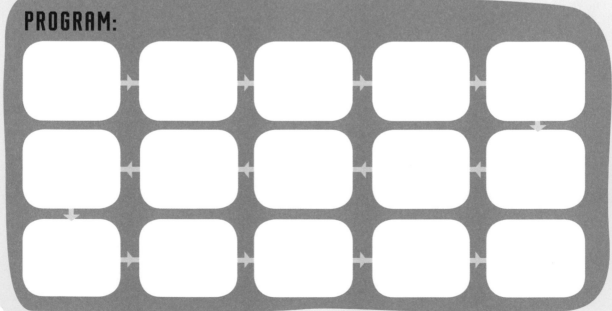

STAYING PUT

Things will stay put unless a force acts on them.
A mug on a table won't move by itself. This is known as INERTIA.

You can demonstrate INERTIA with a simple experiment...

Cut out a strip from a blank sheet of paper, roughly 20cm (8in) long and 5cm (2in) wide. Find a glue stick, or an unbreakable object of a similar size and weight.

Place the strip and your object on a table, like this.

Make sure about half the strip hangs over the edge.

Pull the strip away as QUICKLY as possible.

Try it a few times.

WHAT HAPPENS?

You should find that the movement is so quick, the inertia of the glue stick overcomes the force, so it stays put.

Civil engineers have to consider inertia to make sure buildings stay put, even when forces such as wind and earthquakes are pushing against them.

The heavier the object, the more inertia there is and the harder it is to move.

EARTHQUAKE DETECTOR

How do you measure the strength of an earthquake?

Earthquakes begin at a point underground known as the HYPOCENTRE.

Energy ripples out in all directions in what are known as SEISMIC WAVES...

...making the ground SHAKE back and forth.

For centuries, engineers have built machines to try to measure the STRENGTH of the shaking...

1783: Andrea Bina hung a large ROCK with a POINTER from a ceiling.

Rock, or PENDULUM, stayed relatively still as ground shook

Pointer traced ground movements in tray of sand

THE RESULT: A pattern like this...

LONGER lines meant a STRONGER earthquake, because the ground shook more.

Scribble in the patterns a weak and a strong earthquake would make.

1880: James Ewing invented a device called the HORIZONTAL PENDULUM SEISMOMETER.

It showed how the strength of the shaking changed over TIME.

Pendulum suspended from a special frame that allowed it to stay completely still as ground shook

Indicator recorded ground movements on a revolving glass plate

THE RESULT: A graph like this...

Can you follow the hints to complete the graph?

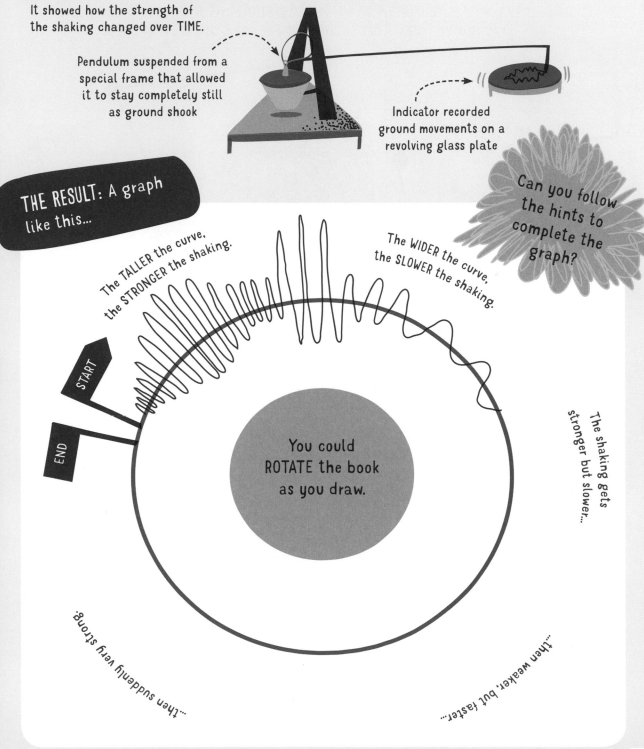

The TALLER the curve, the STRONGER the shaking.

The WIDER the curve, the SLOWER the shaking.

START

END

You could ROTATE the book as you draw.

The shaking gets stronger but slower...

...then weaker, but faster...

...then suddenly very strong.

FACE RECOGNITION

Software engineers can write programs that make computers recognize faces. This technology is used to SOLVE CRIMES.

The computer finds a FACE in an image from the scene of the crime...

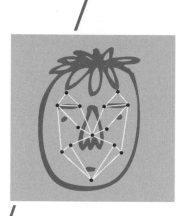

...and connects specific points to make a GRID.

Using grids, the computer compares the face from the scene of the crime to the faces of possible SUSPECTS already on police files.

Like a fingerprint, every human face is UNIQUE. So, if any grids MATCH, it proves that the suspect was at the scene of the crime.

WHO DUNNIT?

A detective has images from a security camera at the scene of a robbery. The burglar's face is blurry, but the computer is able to produce the following grid.

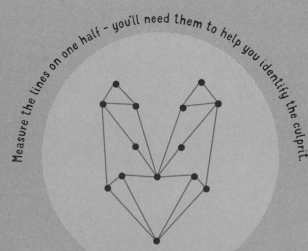

Measure the lines on one half – you'll need them to help you identify the culprit.

Now, connect the points on each suspect's face and
measure the same lines. Can you find a match?

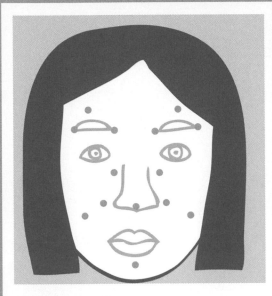

Suspect A

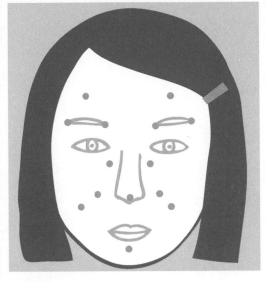

Suspect B

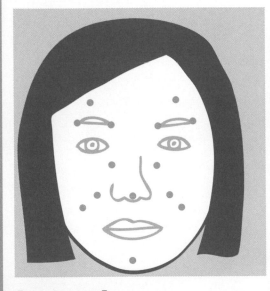

Suspect C

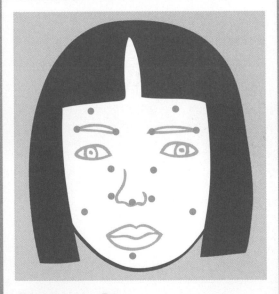

Suspect D

WHO WAS THE BURGLAR? _ _ _ _ _ _ _ _ _ _ _ _ _

See page 78 for
the correct answer.

SPACE JUNK

Man-made debris orbiting Earth is known as space junk.

It includes...

...chunks from damaged satellites.

...discarded rocket boosters.

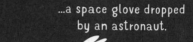
...a space glove dropped by an astronaut.

Space junk travels SO FAST, a chunk the size of your hand could break through the side of a satellite.

Astronautical engineers are working on prototype machines to clear it all up. Here are some of their ideas.

CLEANSPACE ONE

Optical sensors TRACK DOWN junk.

A giant net opens and closes to CATCH junk.

SLING-SAT

Extendable arms CATCH debris in baskets...

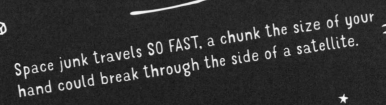

...and HURL it back to Earth, where it burns up in the atmosphere.

The force of the throw PROPELS Sling-Sat on to the next piece of junk.

ATMOSPHERE

Unfortunately, none of the designs so far has worked very well. Can you think of anything else to try? Scribble your ideas here.

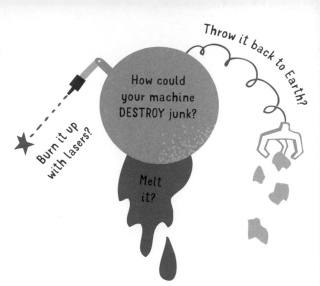

How could your machine DESTROY junk?

Burn it up with lasers?

Throw it back to Earth?

Melt it?

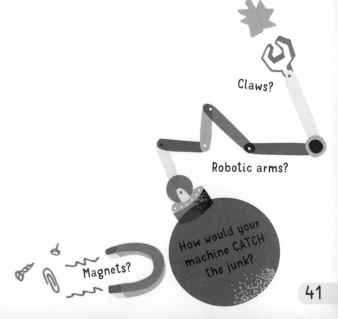

Claws?

Robotic arms?

How would your machine CATCH the junk?

Magnets?

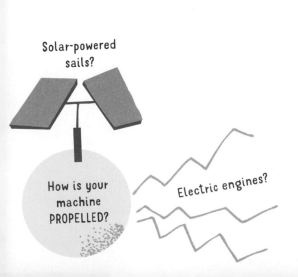

Solar-powered sails?

How is your machine PROPELLED?

Electric engines?

LOOPS, HILLS AND THRILLS

Thanks to engineering, the cars on a roller coaster don't need an engine.

A mechanical lift brings the car to the top of the first hill, then releases it. From then on, TWO types of energy keep the car moving...

START

POTENTIAL ENERGY
A store of energy. The HIGHER the car goes, the MORE potential energy it gains.

KINETIC ENERGY
The energy the car has when it's moving.

Potential energy turns into kinetic energy as the car zooms DOWN a hill...

...and turns back into potential energy when it goes UP again.

But the car won't keep moving forever.

The car LOSES kinetic energy to a force known as FRICTION. This converts kinetic energy into heat and sound as the wheels rub against the track.

HEAT

SOUND

The hills have to be designed to get SMALLER as the car loses energy. Otherwise it won't make it to the finish.

FINISH

DESIGN YOUR OWN ROLLER COASTER

...OR add a mechanical lift, if you want the next hill to be taller.

Make sure the hills and loops get SMALLER as the roller coaster goes on, so your car can reach the finish...

A STEEPER, LONGER drop will give your car MORE kinetic energy.

INFO EXPRESS

When two or more computers are connected together, they form a NETWORK. The largest network in the world is the internet, which allows computers all over the planet to share information.

When a computer sends information or 'data', it's broken into chunks known as PACKETS.

Devices known as ROUTERS pass the data packets along the network.

S1

A device known as a SERVER processes the packets and works out where they need to go.

There are MULTIPLE ROUTES a packet can take.

If part of the network is damaged or switched off...

...the routers find an ALTERNATIVE ROUTE.

S2

Another server sends the packets out to the receiving computer.

When the data packets reach the receiving computer, they're reassembled and the information is shared.

Maintaining computer networks is a job for NETWORK ENGINEERS.

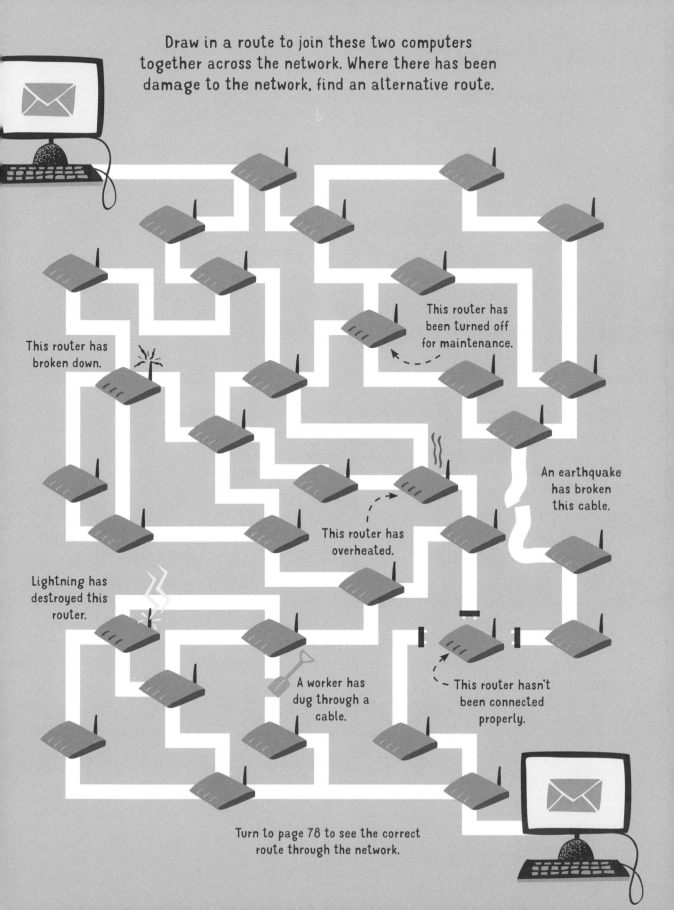

Draw in a route to join these two computers together across the network. Where there has been damage to the network, find an alternative route.

This router has broken down.

This router has been turned off for maintenance.

An earthquake has broken this cable.

This router has overheated.

Lightning has destroyed this router.

A worker has dug through a cable.

This router hasn't been connected properly.

Turn to page 78 to see the correct route through the network.

WARP AND WEFT

Textile engineers design weaving machines, and develop new materials to be woven. Give TEXTILE ENGINEERING a try with this paper weaving project.

Fabric is made up of two key parts – the WARP and WEFT.

Changing the pattern of the weft changes the properties of the fabric.

THE WARP
(yarn stretched lengthwise)

THE WEFT
(yarn woven between the warp)

SEE FOR YOURSELF

Copy the templates on the next page, or print them from the Usborne QUICKLINKS website.

Fold and cut as marked, then weave these patterns.

PLAIN WEAVE

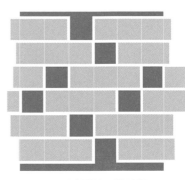

SATIN WEAVE

TEST THEM

WAVE

STRETCH

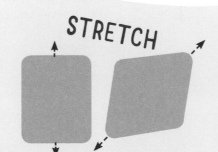

TWIST

Is one more STRETCHY? Which feels STRONGER?

Turn to page 78 to see if we found the same.

CUT OUT
6 STRIPS.

WEFT

1	2	3	4	5	6

MAKING A WARP

Cut out the square along the solid black lines. Fold along the dotted white line, then cut along the solid white lines while still folded (DON'T CUT PAST THE ENDS). Unfold it, and you're ready to start weaving.

FOLD
ALONG
DOTTED
LINE.

CUT
SOLID
LINES
WHILE
FOLDED.

WARP for plain weave

WEFT

FOLD
ALONG
DOTTED
LINE.

CUT
SOLID
LINES
WHILE
FOLDED.

WARP for satin weave

1	2	3	4	5	6

CUT OUT
6 STRIPS.

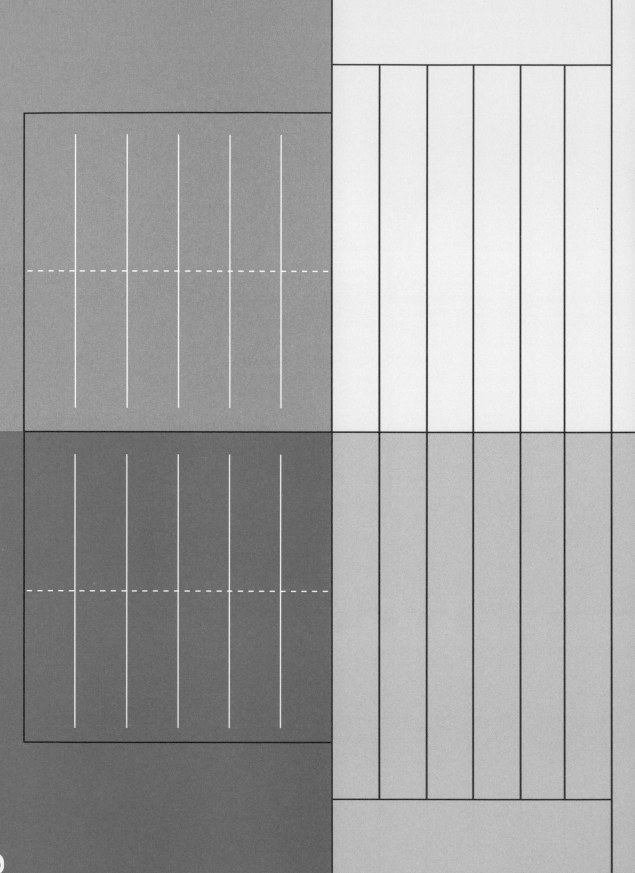

MAPPING THE LAND

Drones can be used to survey land to be built on.

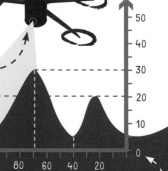

Drone

A camera takes photographs.

Sensors measure altitude.

ALTITUDE (m)

50
40
30
20
10
0

200 180 160 140 120 100 80 60 40 20

Altitude 0 is SEA LEVEL.

THE END RESULT:
An image like this...

Droop

Start and end here.

River

Snodsbury

Ifton

Oddington

Twintle

Buckleswick

Negative numbers are below sea level.

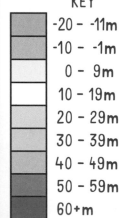

KEY	
	-20 − -11m
	-10 − -1m
	0 − 9m
	10 − 19m
	20 − 29m
	30 − 39m
	40 − 49m
	50 − 59m
	60+m

An engineer is planning a new road that connects all the villages on the map. It has to be built between 10-19m above sea level, because the rest of the terrain is too STEEP.

Plan a possible route. Add in bridges to cross the river.

ARTIFICIAL LIMBS

Biomedical engineers can create artificial limbs, known as PROSTHETICS, to replace limbs lost through accidents or disease. Each limb is specially built to fit the wearer.

DESIGN ONE TO FIT YOU:
Draw around your forearm, then fill it with the components below.

ELECTRODES: Pick up electrical signals from the brain...

...with INSTRUCTIONS such as 'turn wrist' or 'bend fingers'.

SOCKET: Connects prosthetic to the wearer's arm.

Soft lining protects skin

Lightweight shell (usually plastic)

CONTROL UNIT: Sends signals to motors, which make the limb move.

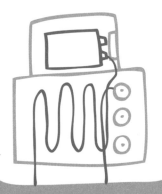

The inside of a prosthetic might look something like this.

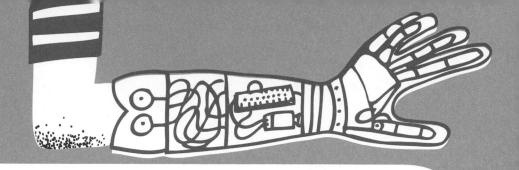

HAND COMPONENTS:

WRIST AND FINGER MOTORS:
Make wrist twist and flex, and fingers bend and straighten.

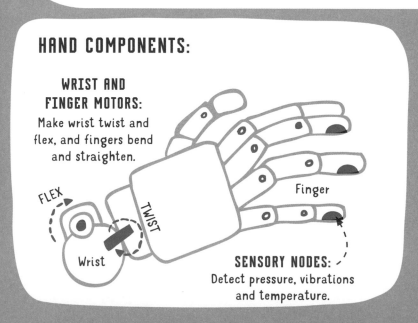

FLEX

TWIST

Wrist

Finger

SENSORY NODES:
Detect pressure, vibrations and temperature.

ANYTHING ELSE YOU CAN THINK OF:

Touchscreen palm?

Light-up fingertips?

THE CYBATHLON

THE CYBATHLON is a competition where BIOMEDICAL and ROBOTICS engineers test inventions that are designed to make the lives of people with physical disabilities easier.

Competitors race to complete challenges. Can you think up inventions to help people who can't walk overcome these three challenges?

CLIMBING THE STAIRS

This is impossible in an ordinary wheelchair...

Adapt a wheelchair?

Give it tracks with grip?

Design a robotic suit?

These are known as POWERED EXOSKELETONS.

CROSSING BUMPY TERRAIN

Some surfaces are UNCOMFORTABLE or DIFFICULT to cross on wheels...

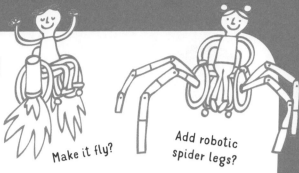

Make it fly?

Add robotic spider legs?

GETTING UP FROM AN ARMCHAIR

This means helping someone to move their legs and stand up...

Use pads that stick to surfaces to pull the user up?

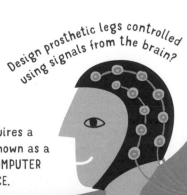

Design prosthetic legs controlled using signals from the brain?

This requires a device known as a BRAIN-COMPUTER INTERFACE.

SAFE LANDINGS

Sending a spacecraft to another planet is hard enough, but it's only part of the problem. Engineers also have to find a way of landing it safely...

When the CURIOSITY ROVER was sent to Mars, engineers used several techniques...

LANDER >>>

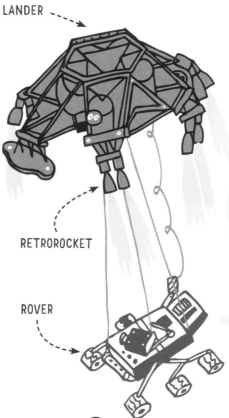

1

The descent began with a PARACHUTE. But parachutes need air to push against, and the air on Mars is very thin...

2

...so the lander used RETROROCKETS – rockets that fire downwards to slow the descent.

RETROROCKET

ROVER

CURIOSITY weighs a massive 900kg (2,000lbs) – more than a fully grown polar bear.

Smaller rovers have used giant air-bags, known as DISPLACEMENT BAGS, to cushion their fall.

3

Once the lander was close enough, the rover was gently lowered onto the surface.

BOUNCE

BOUNCE

4

The lander then flew away to crash land 650m (2,100ft) away.

THIS LANDER IS FALLING TOO FAST!

Scribble on some features to slow it down.
You could use a parachute and retrorockets
or displacement bags, or come up with
a few ideas of your own.

IDEAS

Wings to help
it glide down
safely?

Could it drop a
self-inflating air
mattress for a
soft landing?

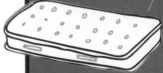

  Springs could
give it some
bounce?

Balloons to help it
float down gently?

WEARABLE TECH

Clothes with built-in technology are known as WEARABLES.

These particular wearables help to keep skiers safe and measure their performance.

GOGGLES: A SCREEN inside uses signals from satellites to display live information to the skier, such as...

JUMP HEIGHT and AIR TIME

SPEED and ALTITUDE

LOCATION

GLOVES:
Built-in HEATERS and BUTTONS to control temperature

WATCH:
Measures wearer's HEART RATE

BACKPACK:
INFLATES in an avalanche, helping to keep wearer from sinking

Invent some wearables to protect hikers in the rainforest against the DANGERS below – or imagine your own dangers.

Below are some ideas to inspire you.

POISONOUS INSECTS

A built-in sensor to detect when insects land on you?

An automatic insect-repellent spray?

GETTING LOST
(easy in dense vegetation)

A belt that works out your location using satellite signals, then directs you?

TURN LEFT

HELP!

A backpack that shoots flares to let others know where you are?

TOPPLING TOWERS

Which of these paper buildings is more likely to be blown over by a gust of wind?

Tall paper apartment block

Small paper house

TAKE A GUESS:

LET'S SEE IF YOU WERE RIGHT.

BUILD IT:

Copy the template on the next page, or print it from the Usborne QUICKLINKS website. Fold and stick the buildings as marked.

TEST IT:

Place the model buildings side by side, then wave this book at them until one falls over.

WHICH TOPPLED FIRST?

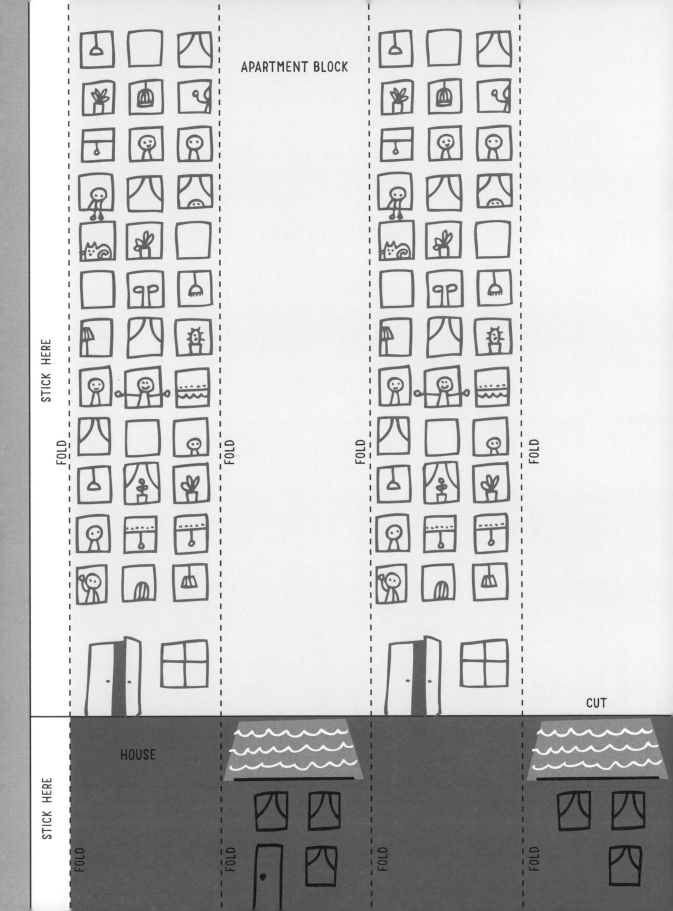

APARTMENT BLOCK

STICK HERE

FOLD

FOLD

FOLD

FOLD

CUT

HOUSE

STICK HERE

FOLD

FOLD

FOLD

FOLD

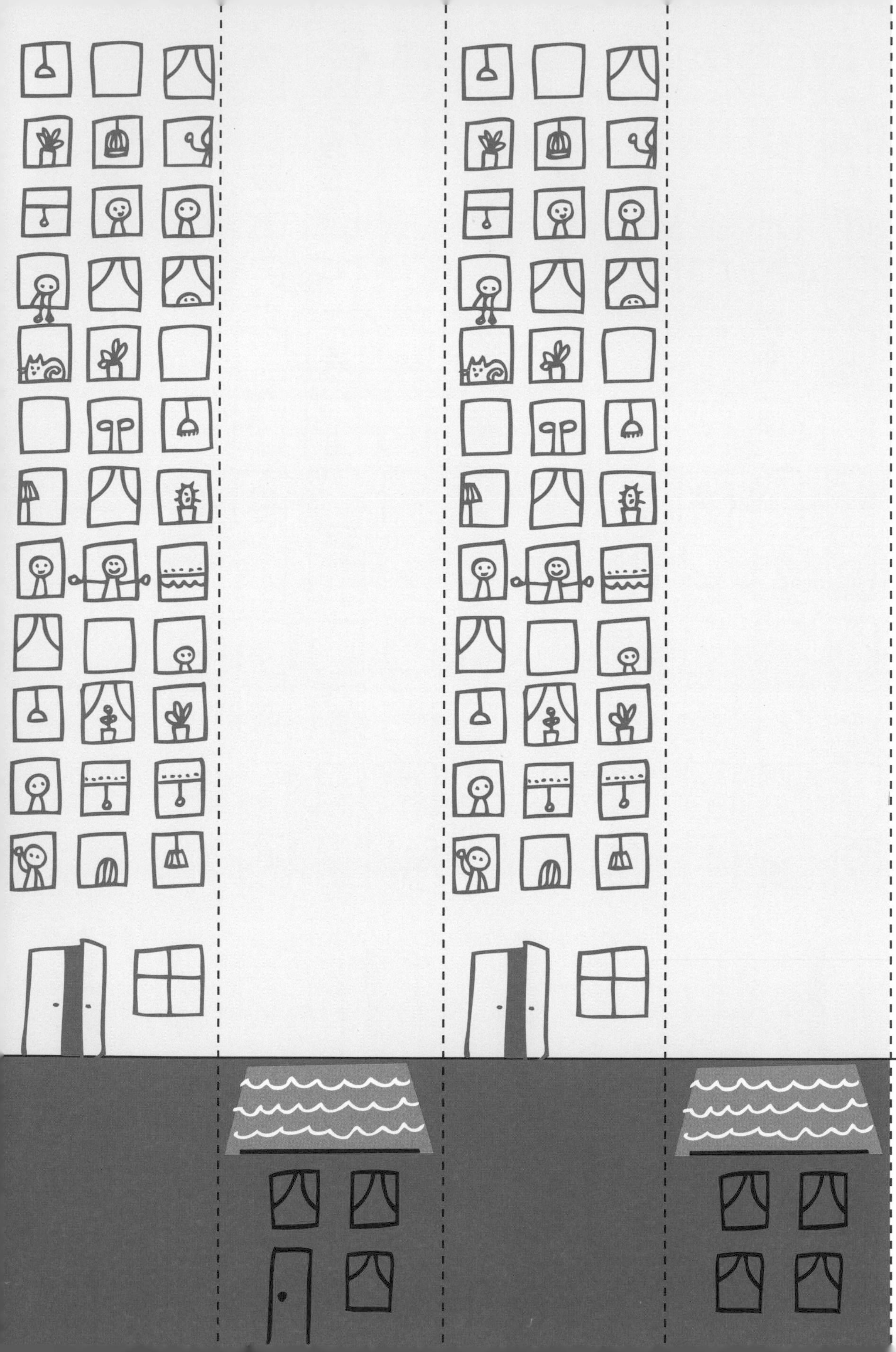

STICK HERE

STICK HERE

The taller building TOPPLES...

...and the smaller one stays upright.

BUT WHY?

The weight of a building balances around an imaginary point, called...

THE CENTRE OF GRAVITY
(marked in red)

All objects have one.

The LOWER the centre of gravity, the more STABLE the building.

The taller paper building has a HIGHER centre of gravity than the shorter one.

MOVING THE CENTRE OF GRAVITY

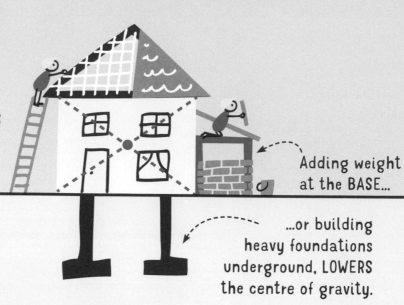

Adding weight to the TOP of a building RAISES the centre of gravity.

Adding weight at the BASE...

...or building heavy foundations underground, LOWERS the centre of gravity.

KEEP IT DOWN

Can you scribble extra parts onto this building to make its centre of gravity lower?

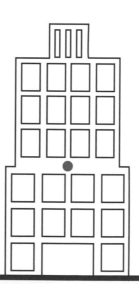

Turn to page 79 to see some of the ways a professional engineer might do it.

GREAT INVENTIONS

Using the clues, can you match the inventors to their inventions?

PERCY SPENCER
Physicist who realized the radar he was working with melted the chocolate in his pocket

GRACE HOPPER
Computer scientist and rear admiral in the US Navy

JOHN LOGIE BAIRD
Worked on sending pictures and sound using radio waves and telephone lines

STEPHANIE KWOLEK
Chemist who worked on developing tough materials

MARY ANDERSON
Inventor who noticed the difficulty that car and tram drivers had seeing in the rain and snow

KEVLAR
A lightweight and incredibly strong material used in bulletproof vests, bicycle wheels, and even tennis rackets

TELEVISION
A device that transmits sound and moving pictures

MICROWAVE OVEN
Uses radiation to heat up food

WINDSCREEN WIPER
A device which clears the windscreen of a vehicle

FLOW-MATIC
The first computer language based on a human language (English), rather than mathematics

1110100111
000101110
101110101

If equal go to Operation 5: Otherwise go to Operation 2.

Turn to page 80 for the answers.

SHORT CIRCUITS

Electrical engineers use simplified drawings known as **CIRCUIT DIAGRAMS** to map out how electricity flows in machines and buildings.

Circuits begin and end at a **POWER SOURCE** – such as a battery.

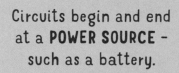

- +

Electricity flows from one end of the battery to the other, along wires.

Items in the circuit, such as bulbs or speakers, are known as **COMPONENTS**.

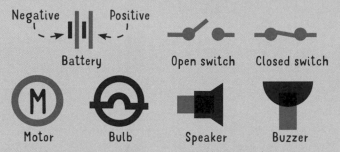

Negative   Positive

Battery   Open switch   Closed switch

Motor   Bulb   Speaker   Buzzer

Circuit diagrams use standard **SYMBOLS** like these to show each component.

This is a very simple circuit, where the switch turns a bulb **ON** or **OFF**.

In this circuit, when **SWITCH 1** is pressed, it sounds a **BUZZER** in a doorbell.

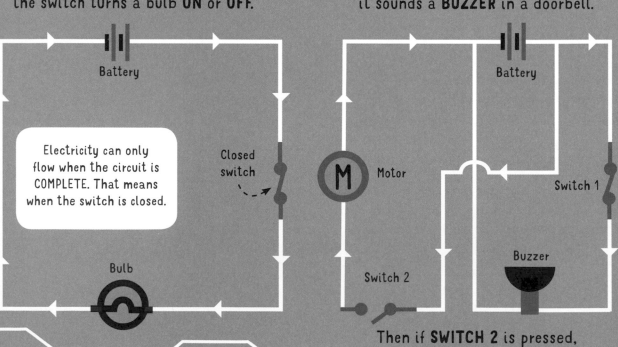

Battery

Electricity can only flow when the circuit is COMPLETE. That means when the switch is closed.

Closed switch

Bulb

Battery

Motor

Switch 1

Switch 2

Buzzer

Then if **SWITCH 2** is pressed, a **MOTOR** opens a door.

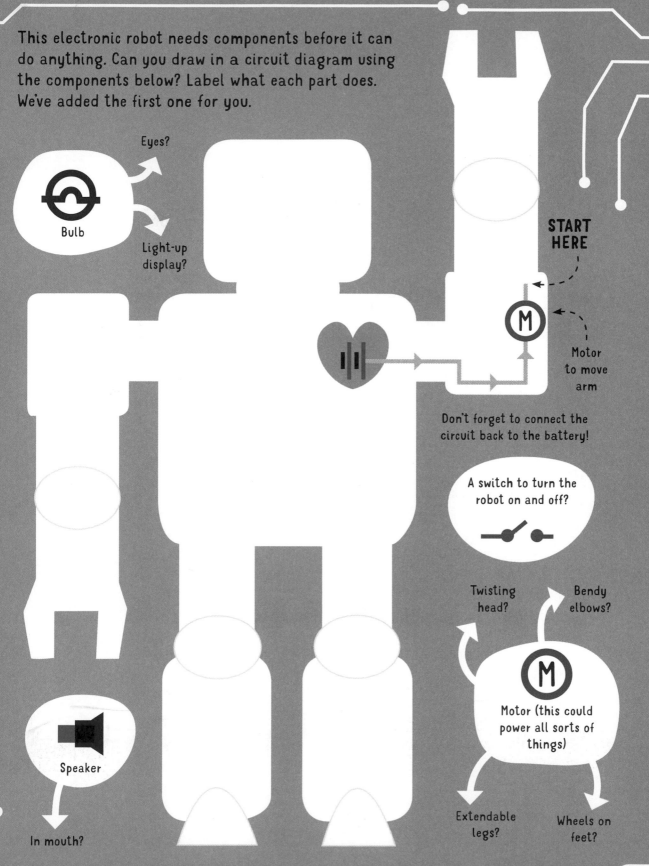

This electronic robot needs components before it can do anything. Can you draw in a circuit diagram using the components below? Label what each part does. We've added the first one for you.

Eyes?

Bulb

Light-up display?

START HERE

M

Motor to move arm

Don't forget to connect the circuit back to the battery!

A switch to turn the robot on and off?

Twisting head?

Bendy elbows?

M

Motor (this could power all sorts of things)

Speaker

In mouth?

Extendable legs?

Wheels on feet?

UP IN THE AIR

Try your hand at aerospace engineering by making a paper plane and helicopter. (Turn to the next page for the helicopter.)

PAPER PLANE

Copy the template on the next page, or print it from the Usborne QUICKLINKS website.

Fold it in half.

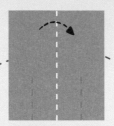

Open it up and fold down the CORNERS.

Fold in the folded edges.

Fold the paper in half, with the previous folds INSIDE.

Fold one side down (along the dotted orange line) to make a WING.

Fold the other side down to make a second wing.

Pull the wings UP level like this, then THROW IT.

What do you see? Throw it a few times and note your observations here.

FLIGHT LOG:

How long did it stay in the air?

Roughly how far did it fly?

How straight (or not) did it fly?

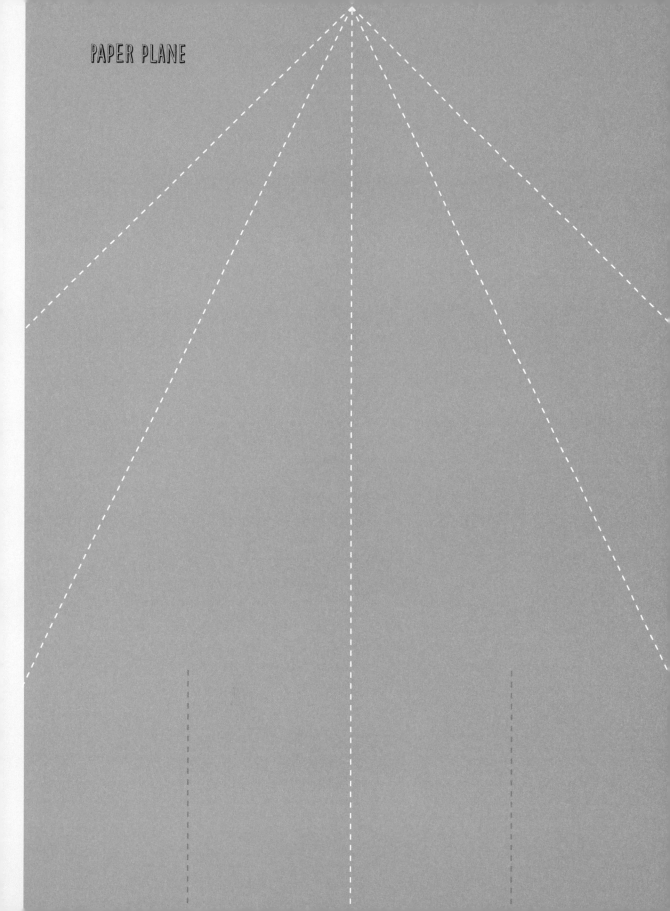

PAPER PLANE

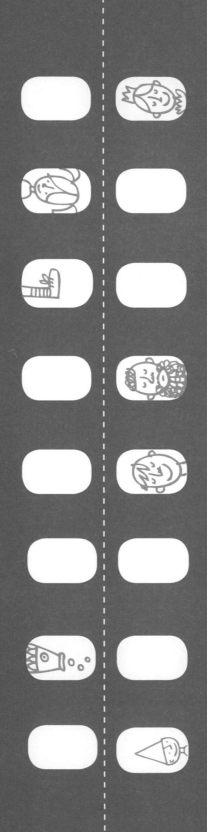

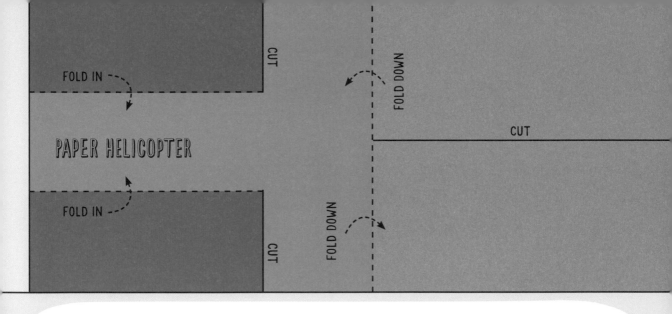

CUT

FOLD IN

FOLD DOWN

PAPER HELICOPTER

CUT

FOLD IN

CUT

FOLD DOWN

PAPER HELICOPTER

Copy the template above, or print it from the Usborne QUICKLINKS website, then...

Cut along the solid lines.

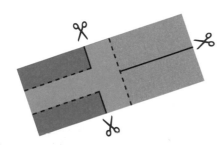

Fold in the red flaps as shown, and fasten with a paperclip.

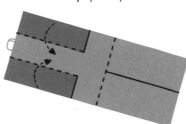

Then fold the blue flaps down to make helicopter BLADES.

Now stand on your tiptoes and DROP IT.

Try it a few times and note your observations here.

FLIGHT LOG:

How long did it stay in the air?

- -

Did it spin? Which way?

- -

Try folding the blades the other way around. Does anything change?

- -

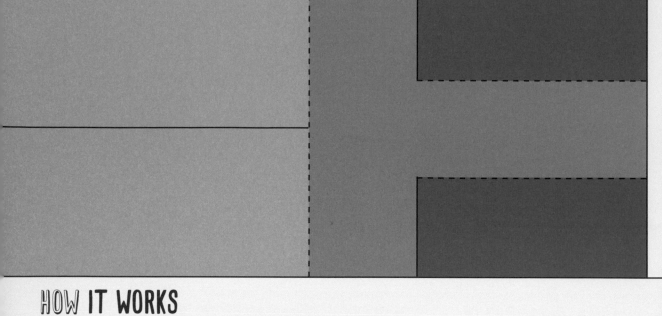

HOW IT WORKS

As the plane glides, air FLOWS AROUND its wings. This helps to keep it up.

As the plane slows, LESS air flows around its wings, and it loses height.

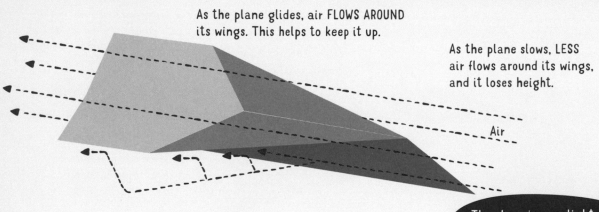

Air

The plane is very light, so a gust of wind may make it suddenly change direction.

As the helicopter falls, air PUSHES against its blades.

Air

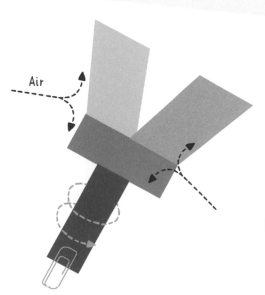

Each blade is pushed in a different direction, making the helicopter spin.

Folding the blades the OTHER way makes the helicopter spin in the OPPOSITE direction.

BEND THE WING TIPS

This changes the way air flows around the wings.

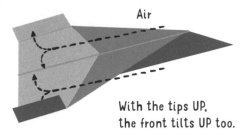

Air

With the tips UP,
the front tilts UP too.

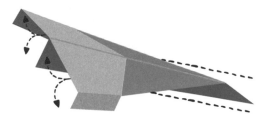

With the tips DOWN,
the front points DOWN.

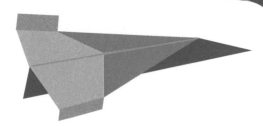

What happens if you bend one tip UP, and the other DOWN?

ADD PAPERCLIPS

This adds more weight, making the air push against the blades with more force.

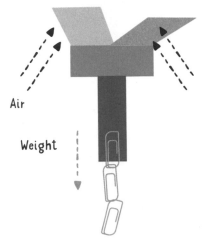

Air

Weight

What happens to the helicopter's spin as you add more paperclips?

- -

If the weight becomes TOO great, the push of the air becomes too strong for the blades...

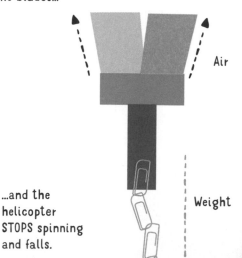

Air

...and the helicopter STOPS spinning and falls.

Weight

Turn to page 80 to see what we found.

SPACE JIGSAW

Building the International Space Station, or ISS, has been one of the MOST ambitious engineering projects ever. The ISS is as big as a football pitch, and weighs 450 times more than a car. This meant that it was TOO BIG to be sent into space in one go. It had to be assembled IN ORBIT instead.

On the ISS you'll find...

...SOLAR PANELS that collect sunlight to give the astronauts electricity.

Design your own space station by scribbling extra parts onto the incomplete space station below.

Add an astronaut on a spacewalk to this TETHER.

Add a telescope for studying Earth from space.

Scribble a SPACECRAFT delivering supplies to the astronauts.

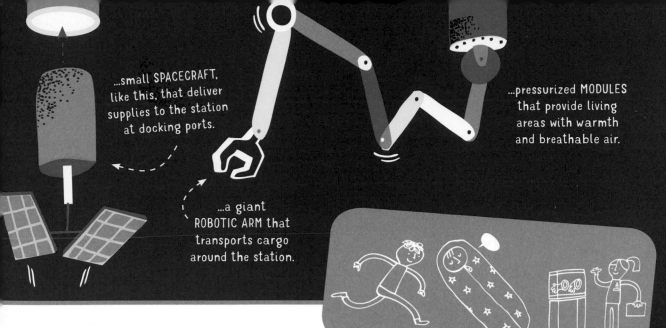

...small SPACECRAFT, like this, that deliver supplies to the station at docking ports.

...pressurized MODULES that provide living areas with warmth and breathable air.

...a giant ROBOTIC ARM that transports cargo around the station.

Attach some modules. What's inside? Science labs? Bedrooms?

Docking port

How about a MODULE with a window for admiring the view? Or somewhere to store cargo and food?

DESIGN FOR THE FUTURE

People throw away around 2 billion tons of waste every year, which is a HUGE problem for the environment. Sustainability engineers try to design products and packaging that produce LESS waste.

HOW?

Using materials that can be RECYCLED easily, such as...

Glass

Aluminium (a metal)

Can be recycled an infinite number of times.

Paper

Cardboard

Can be recycled 5-7 times, but eventually break down (or BIODEGRADE) completely.

Avoiding materials that are DIFFICULT to recycle, such as...

Some types of plastic. They release harmful CHEMICALS during the recycling process.

Clingfilm

Packaging with different materials STUCK TOGETHER. To be recycled, each material has to be separated.

Metal foil ---- Plastic

Designing products and packaging out of parts that can be REUSED...

...AS THEY ARE.

Box for delivering food to supermarkets...

...can be folded up and sent back to warehouse for reuse.

...AS SOMETHING ELSE.

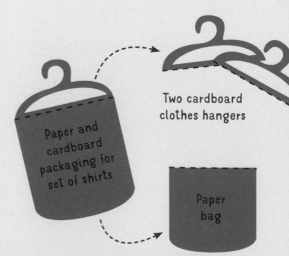

Two cardboard clothes hangers

Paper and cardboard packaging for set of shirts

Paper bag

Disposable plastics are especially bad for the environment.
They are difficult to recycle, and don't biodegrade. If they end up in the
wild or the ocean, they can harm animals and cause chemical pollution.

Can you fill in the table below with ideas for how each plastic product
could be REUSED instead of thrown away, and a RECYCLABLE ALTERNATIVE that
could be used instead? There are suggestions in the table to inspire you.

PRODUCT	REUSE THEM AS...	OR USE THESE INSTEAD...
PLASTIC BOTTLES	...flower pots?	Drinking glasses, or aluminium bottles?
PLASTIC BAGS	...mudguards for shoes?	Biodegradable paper bags?
DRINKING STRAWS	...woven baskets?	Edible straws to eat after use?

14 COLLAPSING COLUMNS

You'll probably find that the CIRCULAR COLUMN is the strongest.

It doesn't have any corners, so the weight you put on top is spread out evenly. That's why columns that hold up buildings are often circular.

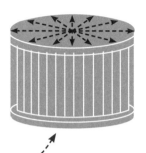

Weight on top of the triangular or square columns gets concentrated in the corners, which become weak points and collapse.

17 COGS in the machine

The first cog needs to turn CLOCKWISE.

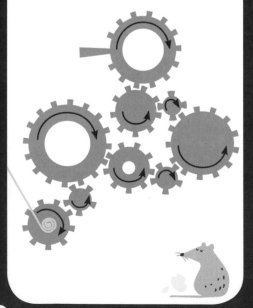

18-19 OH, SO SIMPLE

Pulley

Inclined plane

Wedge

BEFORE   AFTER

Lever

22 BUILDING BRIDGES

You'll probably find that BRIDGE 3 can support the most coins, followed by Bridge 2, then Bridge 1.

When you place a small object on your model, a force PUSHES DOWN on it.

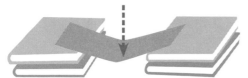

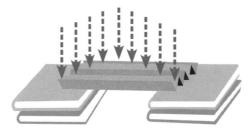

When the paper is FLAT, the force is concentrated on one area. That area has to bear the WHOLE force.

Folding the paper SPREADS the impact of the force along the folded edges, helping to spread it over a LARGER area. The greater the number of folds, the stronger the paper bridge.

25 WATER, WATER EVERYWHERE

   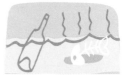

Hilly terrain   Underground river   Canyon   Polluted water

Pumps   Tunnels and pipes   Aqueducts   Water treatment works

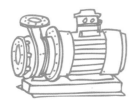   

30 UNDERSEA EXPLORER   Correct program:

33 ROBO-CHEF

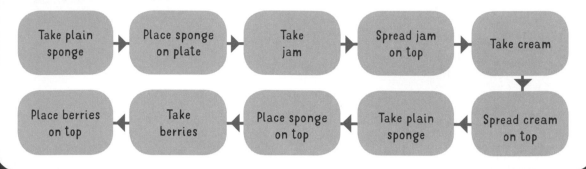

| Take plain sponge | → | Place sponge on plate | → | Take jam | → | Spread jam on top | → | Take cream |

Place berries on top ← Take berries ← Place sponge on top ← Take plain sponge ← Spread cream on top

38-39 FACE RECOGNITION

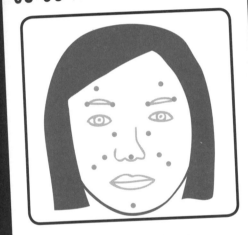

Suspect C was the burglar.

44-45 COMPUTER NETWORKS

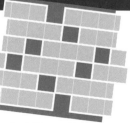

46 WARP AND WEFT

You should find that the plain weave feels STRONGER than the satin...

...but the satin is more FLEXIBLE and STRETCHY than the plain.

This is because there are more points at which the warp and weft overlap in the plain weave, giving each strip of paper less room to move.

58 TOPPLING TOWERS - POSSIBLE SOLUTIONS

1. BUILD HEAVY FOUNDATIONS UNDERGROUND

There are two different categories of building foundation - SHALLOW and DEEP. Some of the differences are explained below.

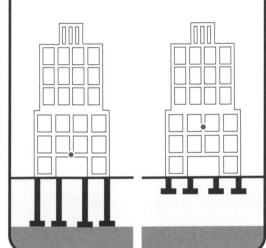

2. ADD WEIGHT AT THE BASE

This means more of the building's weight is concentrated nearer the ground, so the centre of gravity LOWERS. For example, by adding a BASEMENT or widening the bottom floors.

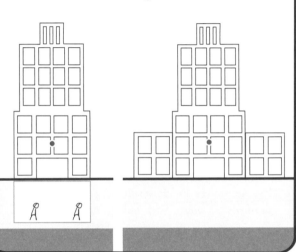

MORE ABOUT FOUNDATIONS

SHALLOW FOUNDATIONS
can be built to depths as little as 1m (3ft). There are several different kinds.

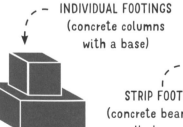

INDIVIDUAL FOOTINGS (concrete columns with a base)

STRIP FOOTINGS (concrete beam below a wall above ground)

RAFT FOUNDATIONS
(large concrete slab beneath a building that supports multiple walls)

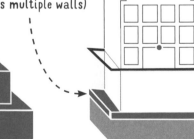

DEEP FOUNDATIONS
go deep enough to reach a layer of rock or sturdy soil. This TRANSFERS the weight of the building to the rock to stop it from SINKING, and LOWERS the centre of gravity to make the building STABLE. Some very tall buildings have foundations as deep as 65m (200ft).

63 INVENTORS AND INVENTIONS

STEPHANIE KWOLEK

Kevlar

PERCY SPENCER

Microwave oven

GRACE HOPPER

FLOW-MATIC

JOHN LOGIE BAIRD

Television

MARY ANDERSON

Windscreen wiper

71 UP IN THE AIR

If one wing tip is up and the other is down, the air pushes the downwards tip up, and the upwards tip down. This makes the plane veer sideways, or roll over completely.

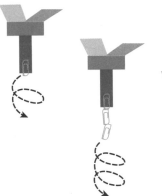

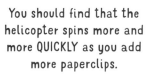

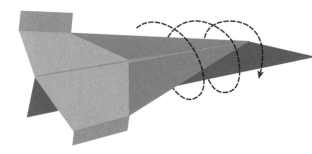

You should find that the helicopter spins more and more QUICKLY as you add more paperclips.

Photographic credits: p.28 - Burdock seed pod, SEM © Dennis Kunkel Microscopy/Science Photo Library; SEM of a hooks and loops fastner © Dr Jeremy Burgess/Science Photo Library; Shark skin SEM © Eye of Science/Science Photo Library; 3D printed shark skin © Miranda Waldron/University of Cape Town.

Many thanks to the CYBATHLON team/ETH ZURICH for permission to mention the CYBATHLON on pages 54-55.

First published in 2018 by Usborne Publishing Ltd., Usborne House, 83-85 Saffron Hill, London EC1N 8RT, England. www.usborne.com. Copyright © 2018 Usborne Publishing Ltd.